$1—

To Joan
& Lee
from

The Temple
at Jerusalem:
a Revelation

John Michell

The Golden Gate on its outer, eastern side. It has long been sealed shut, and a Jewish prophecy says that "it shall not be opened until the eyes of Israel shall be opened in the future redemption".

The Temple
at Jerusalem:
a Revelation

John Michell

GOTHIC IMAGE
PUBLICATIONS

The right of John Michell to be identified as the Author of the Work has been
asserted by him in accordance with the Copyright, Designs and Patents Act 1988

First published in Great Britain in 2000 by Gothic Image Publications.
This edition published in 2000 by Gothic Image Publications, PO Box 2568,
Glastonbury, Somerset BA6 8XR, England.

ISBN 0 906362 51 2

A CIP catalogue record for this book is available from the British Library.

A limited edition in hardback, signed and numbered by the author is also
published by Gothic Image Publications.

ISBN 0 906362 49 0

Book design by Richard Adams Associates
Typeset in Didot
Printed in United States of America

Contents

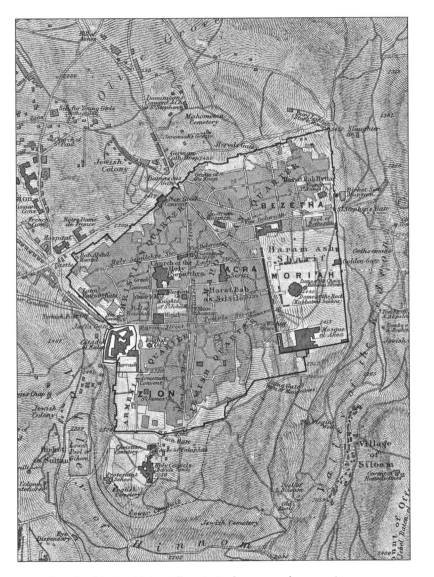

Jerusalem, the old city with its walls, principal streets, and sanctuaries.

Solomon's Temple, its reappearance

ERE IS SOME STARTLING NEWS, which is also
very good news – for many people the best
news that they could possibly hope to hear. It
concerns that disturbed and controversial
part of the world, which is called Israel, Palestine, the
Holy Land and the Near or Middle East. In particular it
is about that most controversial and mysterious building,
the Temple at Jerusalem, founded by King Solomon in
the tenth century BC, destroyed by the armies of Babylon
in 587 BC and rebuilt by the Jews who returned to
Jerusalem after the captivity. King Herod replaced it with
a new, larger temple, commonly called the Second
Temple, a few years before the birth of Christ. This
magnificent structure took many years to build, and it
was barely completed by 70 AD when it was demolished
by the Romans. So thoroughly was it obliterated that no
trace of it remains above ground, and in the course of
time even the place where it stood was forgotten.

That was the situation until recently. It was an
awkward and dangerous situation, awkward for the
religious Jews who are instructed by their law to rebuild
the Temple, and dangerous because the walled platform
around the site is entirely controlled by the Muslims.
Their most holy shrines in the country are located on the
Temple Mount (also called Mount Moriah and Haram al-
Sharif), including the great Aqsa mosque and the sacred
rock beneath the golden dome, Jerusalem's most famous
landmark. Any attempt to excavate for the site of the lost

Temple, let alone set about rebuilding it, would be so fiercely opposed by the whole Muslim world that total and calamitous war would be the likely outcome.

This question of rebuilding the Temple is not just of theoretic or historical interest but immediate and urgent. For the Jews, the necessity of undertaking that task as soon as possible is emphasized by the stern dictum that "a generation that does not rebuild the Temple is judged as if it had destroyed it". This is taken seriously by the religious, and fanatically by certain extremists, who would like to seize the sanctuary area, demolish the Muslim architecture and start construction. A first step to this would be to blow up the golden Dome, exposing at Sakhra, the sacred rock beneath it. This rock is at the centre of Jerusalem's mysteries. Abraham bound Isaac for sacrifice upon it, and it is the rock from which Mohammed ascended to heaven while travelling from Mecca and back in one night. A mark on its surface is identified as the hoofmark of al Burak, Mohammed's flying horse who carried him on the miraculous journey. It has been sanctified from pagan times. Some believe that this rock is the Even Shettiyah, the Rock of Foundation, that stood at the centre of the world in the Holy of Holies within Solomon's Temple. Alternatively, it was the rock of sacrifice. It is also identified as the threshing floor that King David purchased from Ornan the Jesubite after an angel had appeared on it (1 Chronicles, 20). Some of these legends are contradictory, but the fact of their existence shows that this is not a rock to be trifled with.

The good news, completely changing the situation, transcending all difficulties, fulfilling every religious duty and delightful to every inhabitant and lover of Jerusalem, is that the peaceful restoration of the Temple is now actually in process. This is no metaphor or poetic fancy but a physical, concrete fact. Yet no demolition or construction is required, for the site of the Temple has been disclosed, and there it is, fashioned by the ancient builders as that temple of all people, prophesied by Isaiah.

In the following pages the Temple is carefully displayed, allowing everyone with a serious interest in the subject to consider the evidence and decide for themselves on its implications Anyone can see the structure, and religious people will recognize it as the temple referred to in both Jewish and Christian prophecy, which descends ready-made from heaven. There is no need to build it, because here it stands, revealed.

A view of Jerusalem looking west from the Mount of Olives, by Thomas Allom, 1845.
The two blocked doorways of the Golden gate are near the centre of the outer wall,

and within the city stands the Dome of the Rock with the Aqsa mosque to its left.
The pinnacle of Absalom's tomb is seen beyond the figures in the left foreground.

The Temple and the Millennium

There are good, practical reasons for Zionism and the return of the Jews to the Holy Land, but there are also mystical reasons, and these are the deepest and most compelling. A constant theme in Biblical prophecy is that one day the Temple will be seen once more, greater and more splendid than any that preceded it. This will inaugurate the Millennial process, leading to the reunion at Jerusalem of all the twelve tribes of Israel and finally to the reappearance of divine order upon earth.

This does not now seem a likely prospect, certainly not from a political point of view. But we are not here concerned with politics or with any other form of human contrivance, for the great changes that take place in history and human consciousness are not planned but occur spontaneously, as if in accordance with certain universal patterns and cycles. That is indeed the traditional view. Plato and other ancient philosophers attributed the origin of each nation's culture to divine revelation from some god or goddess who gave them their code of law. For as long as they upheld it, strictly, without change or deviation, their lives were long and happy. Human nature, however, is not constant, and everything on earth is subject to entropy and corruption. Observations became lax, innovations crept in, and the societies founded on divine principles either dissolved or were destroyed.

That was the end of one cycle but it was also the beginning of another. The process is illustrated in St

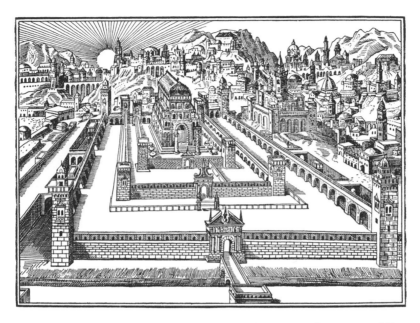

Jerusalem and The Temple in glory. A Hebrew text below prays for its return. "The form of the Temple and the city of Jerusalem, may it be speedily rebuilt and established in our day, Amen, may it be Thy will."

John's Revelation, where the fall of corrupt, mercantile Babylon is followed by the appearance of the Heavenly Jerusalem and a new world of innocence and enlightenment. Divine revelation, of which the Temple is both a symbol and a product, is not just something that may have happened in the past, but ever living, recurring at different times in response to needs, desires, prayers or its own mysterious cycles. These present times are characterized by signs that traditionally signify the end of an era. They are also times of revelation, when the reappearance of Jerusalem's Temple seems no less likely than any future conceived of by economists or politicians.

When the Temple was dedicated by King Solomon it was filled with a dense cloud in which appeared the Glory of the Lord – I Kings, 8, 10-11. There was no need for the censers which the artist, E.S. Hardy, has added to the scene.

The pattern of the Temple

It is not only the Jews who long to see the Temple at Jerusalem restored. Christians have inherited that aspiration with the Old Testament, and it has been the declared purpose of many western idealists and esoteric movements. The crusading Templars and the Knights of St John were dedicated to rebuilding Solomon's Temple, and so today are the Freemasons, who claim King Solomon as their first Master.

Evidently there is more to this than meets the eye. Rebuilding the Temple is not just a construction work but an ideal symbol, corresponding to the Holy Grail, a symbol of paradise again on earth. In the days of Solomon and while the Temple was still intact, the tribes of Israel were prosperous and high-spirited and lived harmoniously in a state of perfect order, as if under divine governance. All this was a product of the Temple and the cycle of rituals performed in and around it. When the Temple was destroyed, they say, the world fell into disorder and nothing has ever gone right since.

Legends of the Temple describe it as the instrument of a mystical, priestly science, a form of alchemy by which oppositely charged elements in the earth and atmosphere were brought together and ritually married. The product of their union was a spirit that blessed and sanctified the people of Israel. In the Holy of Holies dwelt the Shekhinah, the native goddess of the land of Israel. It was her marriage chamber, entered at certain seasons by the bridegroom. His name was the Glory of the God of Israel, and he came from the east, from over the Mount of Olives. He penetrated the Holy of Holies while Solomon was dedicating the Temple (I Kings, 8, 10-11), and in Ezekiel, 43 is a description of his coming.

"Behold, the glory of the God of Israel came from the way of the east: and his voice was like a noise of many waters: and the earth shined with his glory... And the glory of the Lord came into the house by way of the gate whose prospect is toward the east... and, behold, the glory of the Lord filled the house."

Procuring the sacred marriage was a highly technical and potentially dangerous operation. It was not only a work of physics and astronomy but more comprehensive, on the level of *kadesh*, the holy. Every detail of the ceremony had to be followed to the letter. The appropriate sacrifices and burnings, the purifications, processions and chants of the priests, their robes and regalia were strictly specified in Jewish Temple law. Most important were the numbers, measures and harmonies expressed in the dimensions of the Temple. It was built to a certain pattern, reflecting the ideal order of the heavens (the macrocosm) which is also that of the human microcosm. In the Biblical account (I Chronicles, 28, 11-19) it is said that the pattern was given to King David by God himself, in writing, and David passed it on to his son, Solomon, who built his temple according to the divine specifications.

The importance of the Temple's plan is emphasized by the prophets of Israel. Ezekiel goes into it in great detail, giving the dimensions of its various parts as imparted to him by an angel with a measuring rod. "Thou son of man", cried the angel, "Show the house to the house of Israel, that they may be ashamed of their iniquities: and let them measure the pattern." A similar angel, also with a measuring rod, appeared to St John in Revelation, 11, and told him to "rise and measure the temple of God, and the altar, and them that worship therein." The object of his measuring was the celestial Jerusalem, that pattern in the heavens which he saw descending to earth.

The essence of the temple was its plan, and that plan was divinely revealed. It was not a once-and-for-all revelation but is renewed from time to time, and when that happens a new world appears. In the plan of the temple is the key to forgotten knowledge, to the blueprint by which the universe was made, to the lost canon of number, measure and music that provided laws and standards for the Egyptians and other ancient civilizations. That is why the Templars and other mystical idealists devoted lives to discovering the secrets of the Temple. It is like the philosopher's stone, a talisman that turns base metal into gold, that brings new light into the world and restores it to its natural condition as an earthly paradise.

The finding of the old Temple

The question of exactly where on the Temple Mount the former Temple of the Jews was located is controversial and keenly debated. By the seventh century, when the followers of Mohammed took over the Jerusalem sanctuary, the actual site had been forgotten, and even then there were rival theories on its location. Rabbinical scholars believe that Herod built the Second Temple on Solomon's foundations, and most authorities accept that there was only one temple site. Today there are three major theories about where the Temple stood, each of them backed up by plausible evidence. The three hypothetical temples are ranged neatly in a row, one lying over the Dome of the Rock, one to the north of it and the other to the south. All three are virtually parallel and of similar size, with the entrance to the east and the main temple building (the Hekhal) containing the Holy of Holies at the west.

A radically different view on the matter is held by the Muslim custodians of the sanctuary area. They point out that Solomon and David are mythological figures, recorded only by tradition, and that there is no conclusive evidence that the original Temple stood within the walled enclosure. It could have been elsewhere in the city. It is easy to see and sympathize with one motive behind this attitude, which is to discourage Jewish interest in Islam's most sacred precinct. But the case for the Temple in its traditional location is quite formidable. In denying it the Muslim authorities also deny that there is any need for archaeological research in the area. That is why there is such room for doubts and different theories.

Of the three proposed Temple sites two are embarrassing because, if either were accepted, it would involve the Jews in a direct claim to sites of major importance to the Muslims, including the Dome of the Rock. The traditional belief, that the Temple overlaid the Dome site is still held by many scholars. The Rock, al Sakhra, the outcropping peak of Mount Moriah, is identified in the Bible and by Josephus as Solomon's altar of sacrifice. In that case it would have stood in an open courtyard in front of the main temple building. An alternative view, that it stood within the Holy of Holies, is untenable because of its size; measuring some 55 by 40 feet, it would not have fitted into the 20-cubit (34.56 ft.) cube of the sanctum. When the Crusaders held Jerusalem in the twelfth century they accepted the Rock as the pivot of Solomon's works and renamed the Muslim dome as the Temple of Solomon.

Another old belief is that the Temple site is in the south-western quarter of the Haram, somewhere in between the Dome and the Aqsa mosque. This theory is vigorously promoted by the Israeli architect, Tuvia Sagiv. Lengthy researches have convinced him the the Holy of Holies was near the site of al Kas, a sacred Muslim fountain situated north of the mosque. This accords with the tradition that the Jews' sacred place, the Western (formerly Wailing) Wall was the western wall of the Temple precinct.

Passing down the length of Sagiv's temple site is the main east-west line in Jerusalem's street pattern. The Romans called it the Decumanus and built a wide road along the western stretch of it, running eastward from the Jaffa gate along the line of the ancient First wall of David's city. East of the Temple Mount, in the Kidron valley, the terminus of this line is marked by the north side of a prominent, 45-foot-tall monument known as Absalom's Tomb. It is said in the Bible (II Samuel, 18, 18) that Absalom, King David's son, erected a pillar there as a monument to himself. The present structure was probably built in Herodian times during the first century B.C. The distance from the corner of the tower at the Jaffa gate to Absalom's Tomb is 2000 cubits, measured by that cubit of 1.728 feet (0.526694 metres) by which the Temple was built.

The Holy of Holies in Sagiv's temple would have been located on this line, about twenty cubits to the north of al Kas, the large bowl below which is a spring of water. This agrees with Ezekiel, 47, where it is said that waters entered the Temple from the south and then flowed eastwards.

The third contender in the debate is Dr Asher Kaufman of Jerusalem, a physicist, a rabbi and by origin a Scotsman. In 1977 he published a paper, 'New light upon Zion: the plan and precise location of the Second Temple' – a challenging claim. He began, as everyone does, with the Bible texts, and noted in Ezekiel, 8, 16, the prophet's view of the Jerusalem Temple, shown to him in a vision, where he saw "about five and twenty men, with their backs towards the temple of the Lord, and their faces toward the east; and they worshipped the sun toward the east". This confirms that the Temple was orientated eastward towards the Mount of Olives.

Another clue was found in Numbers, 19, which describes the ritual sacrifice of the red heifer. This took place on the Mount of Olives. Verse 4 says that the priest must sprinkle the blood of the heifer "directly before the tabernacle of the congregation seven times". Further details are given in the Mishnah, a collection of old Jewish texts describing laws and customs during and after the Second Temple period. It records that the walls of the Temple were all high, except the wall to the east which was lower, "so that the priest who burnt the red heifer might, while standing on the Mount of Olives, by directing his gaze carefully, see the entrance of the Hekhal [the main temple building] at the time of the sprinkling of the blood". The place of sacrifice must therefore have been on the eastward extension of the Temple's axis, near the summit of the Mount of Olives. By further study of archaeological records and relics, Kaufman was able to identify the probable site of the red heifer sacrifice, to fix the line of the Temple's axis and to discover the original ground-plan of the building.

Kaufman's Temple site, about 100 yards north of the Dome of the Rock, is not occupied by any important Muslim buildings. The only thing on it is a small, pillared structure of sixteenth-century origin, with a dome covering a flat, exposed patch of bedrock. It is called the Dome of the Winds or of the Spirits, and it was formerly

The monument know as Absalom's Tomb played a key part in the geomantic design of Jerusalem in the Herodian period. It marks the eastern end of the 2000-cubit line

to the corner of the tower at the Jaffa gate, defining the southern side of the greater temple rectangle.

The Dome of the Spirits or of the Tablets covers an outcrop of rock on the site of the Holy of Holies in the former Temple. Behind it to the south is the Dome of the Rock built in 691.

known as the Dome of the Tablets. This implies that the two Tablets of the Covenant, given to Moses, once rested there, and therefore that this was the site of the Holy of Holies. When Kaufman matched his reconstructed plan of the Temple with the modern site plan, he was amazed to find that the Holy of Holies in his diagram was on the spot occupied by the Dome of the Tablets. The rock protected by it must then surely be the Rock of Foundation in the inner sanctum of the Temple.

Kaufman's discovery is of the Second Temple, built by King Herod on Solomon's original site but with a different orientation. His conclusion is that Herod's temple faced due east whereas the First Temple was angled about six degrees to the north of east. This is a well worked-out theory, but it may not be correct. Later evidence shows that Herod's orientation was about 5 degrees north of east, and that this was followed by the Roman augers who planned Aelia Caoitolina, The axis of Solomon's temple is likely to have run parallel to the southern wall of the Temple enclosure at 10 degrees north of east.

Sagiv agrees with Kaufman's location of an ancient sacred building at the Dome of the Spirits but believes that it was one of the shrines to native deities which Solomon built together with his Temple. In the latter part of his life, and at the behest of his 700 wives and 300 concubines of many different nations, Solomon turned to the worship of pagan gods and goddesses (I Kings, 11). He dedicated shrines to them and included them within his Temple scheme. This arrangement lasted for a long time, until the sixth century BC when, according to the account in II Kings, 23, King Josiah desecrated Solomon's pagan sanctuaries to the north of the Temple.

Further examination of Kaufman's temple plan and its axis from the Mount of Olives leads to a discovery of greater magnitude than any temple, while settling the question of where the Temple stood and whether it is necessary to build a new one.

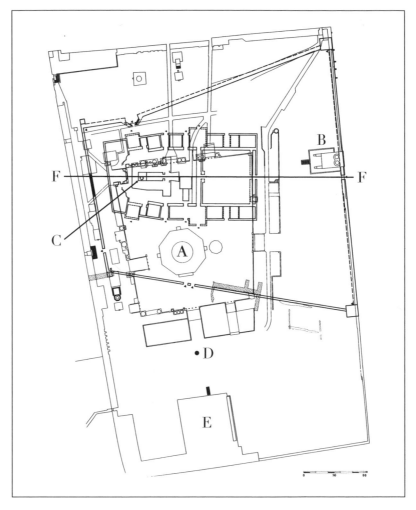

The Temple stood within the Haram al-Sharif, the great walled court completed by Herod the Great in about 20 BC. At its centre is the outcropping peak of Mount Moriah, forming the sacred rock now enclosed by the Muslim Dome. Superimposed on this modern plan is Asher Kaufman's outline of the Second Temple, with its side-chambers and outer court. He locates it to the north of the Dome of the Rock (A) and to the west of the Golden gate (B). Its Holy of Holies overlies the rock now beneath the Dome of the Spirits (C). Other features: D. al-Kas, the Muslim ritual fountain; E. al-Aqsa Mosque. F-F marks the east-west axis of the Second Temple as Kaufman defines it, differing from the 'messianic axis' by some 5 degrees.

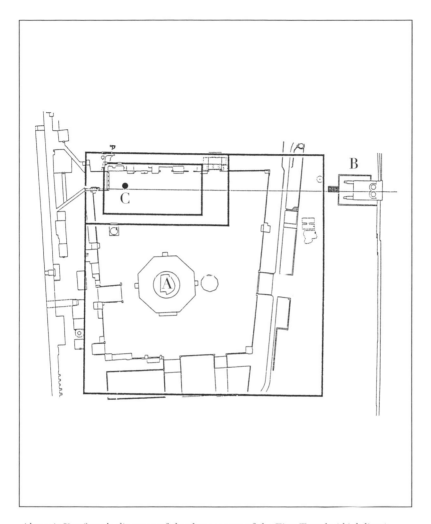

Above is Kaufman's diagram of the three courts of the First Temple (thick lines) showing the axis aligned upon the centre of the Golden gate.

The messianic axis

The line passing down the length of the temple that Kaufman discovered, begins on the Mount of Olives near the traditional site of Jesus's Ascension, enters the Temple Mount along the southern edge of its eastern gate, the famous Golden gate, and then crosses the Dome of the Tablets and the rock within the former Holy of Holies. In 1987 Dr G.S.P. Freeman-Grenville, writer and expert on old Jerusalem, noticed something further: that this same line, extended westwards forms the main axis of the northern quarters of the Old City, conforming to the same grid as the Cardo, the Decumanus and the streets aligned with them. Most remarkably, it runs straight to the rock pinnacle, Golgotha in the Church of the Holy Sepulchre, the rock on which Jesus was crucified. It therefore links the two most sacred rocks and symbolic world-centres of both Jews and Christians.

This invisible line has an awesome reputation. It is described in legends as if it were a tightrope, "as thin as a hair, as sharp as a sword and as black as night", stretching from the Mount of Olives over the valley to the Golden gate. Along it the souls of the righteous pass to their reward in the Holy City. The first to enter are those buried on the Mount of Olives, which is why grave plots on its slope are so highly valued. The traditions of all three religions agree that this is the line on which the Messiah will enter the city. The Jews' story is that, when the Temple was destroyed, the Shekhinah, the divine presence that inhabited the Holy of Holies, left through

Only one door, from a courtyard to the south, gives entrance to the ever-dilapidated Church of the Holy Sepulchre. The rock of Golgotha stands just inside it to the right. This traditional site of the crucifixion and burial of Jesus is divided between several different and often rival churches who are always at loggerheads over their rights and liabilities for repairs. Order is maintained by an hereditary Muslim doorkeeper who holds the keys.

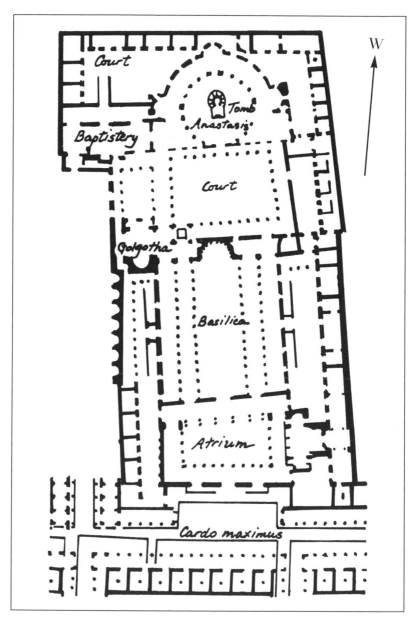

W

Plan of the Holy Sepulchre church, as built by Constantine in the fourth century. The church replaced a Roman temple to Venus which concealed the traditional site of Jesus's tomb. Golgotha stood in a corner of the court, approached by an aisle from the east.

the Golden gate, and that when it is restored she will
enter again that way – on the same line as the Messiah
will take. Christians say the same about Jesus at his
Second Coming, and the New Testament records him as
having already followed that route. On the first Palm
Sunday, he rode along it into Jerusalem from the Mount
of Olives, through the Golden gate and straight into the
Temple, where he kicked out the money-dealers. Shortly
afterwards, he was conducted further along that same
line, to Golgotha where he was crucified.

The Muslim prophecy is that on the Day of
Judgment the angel Gabriel will sound three blasts on a
ram's horn to announce the Resurrection. All the
peoples of the world will assemble on the Mount of
Olives, where Abraham, Moses, Jesus and Mohammed
will stand beside the scales of justice. The souls of those
who have been granted eternal life will pass along the
tightrope and in through the Golden gate.

At one time, during the Second Temple period, a
section of this spiritual, messianic line was marked by a
processional structure. A bridge or causeway supported
by arches ran from the Golden gate across the Kidron
valley. It was called the Causeway of the Heifer, since the
High Priest used it to reach the Mount of Olives where
the ritual burning of the Red Heifer took place.

The ancient Golden gate (also called the Mercy gate,
the Shushan gate, the Eastern gate and, in the New
Testament, the Beautiful gate) is believed to have been
built in about the seventh century, on the foundations of
Herod's larger and more splendid gate which replaced

Solomon's. For reasons partly connected with the messianic prophecies it has been sealed shut for hundreds of years, ever since the Saracens conquered Jerusalem in 1187. A Muslim graveyard is now planted across its entrance. This blocking of the Golden Gate seems to be an old tradition from the time of the First Temple, for Ezekiel, 44, 1-3, records it:

"Then he brought me back by the way of the gate of the outward sanctuary which looketh towards the east; and it was shut.

Then said the Lord unto me; This gate shall be shut, it shall not be opened, and no man shall enter in by it; because the Lord, the God of Israel, hath entered in by it, therefore it shall be shut.

It is for the prince; the prince, he shall sit in it to eat bread before the Lord; he shall enter by the way of the porch of that gate, and shall go out by way of the same."

In early Christian times, the path of Jesus's last journey through the Golden gate, into the Temple and eventually to crucifixion at Golgotha, was made sacred by his followers. When the Crusaders held Jerusalem, they opened the Gate only on Palm Sunday to allow processions. The messianic axis was probably the original route of the Via Dolorosa. One of the last people to have walked along it was the Emperor Heraclius. In 631 he brought back to Jerusalem the fragments of the True Cross which he had regained from the Persians. He carried the relics in a procession along the path taken by

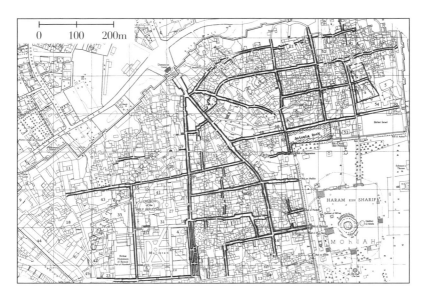

Erich Cohn's reconstruction from archaeological evidence of Jerusalem's street pattern in Roman times. Some of the streets were at least three times wider than they are today, and their paving stones are up to twenty feet below the modern surface.

Jesus from the Mount of Olives, through the Golden gate and on to Golgotha which at that time stood in a courtyard outside the Church of the Holy Sepulchre. In the Church the remains of the Cross were enshrined, together with the cup from the Last Supper, the famous 'spear of destiny' and other relics of the Crucifixion. It is easy to see a reference to this line in Zechariah, 1, 16: "Thus saith the Lord; I am returned to Jerusalem with mercies; my house shall be built on it, saith the Lord of hosts, and a line shall be stretched forth upon Jerusalem."

It has always been an esoteric line, a mythological path rather than a secular highway. It is not a unique line but one of many that are known everywhere as spirit

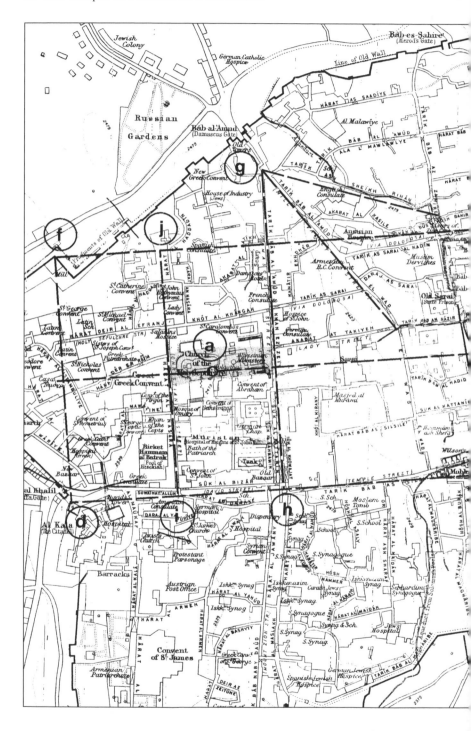

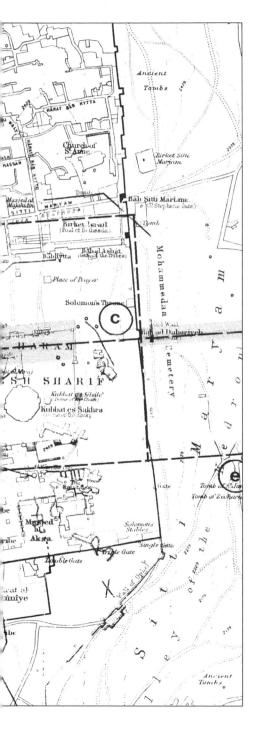

The *'messianic line'* through the Old City, and the two lines parallel to it on either side, form a rectangle with its western end marked by the line between the tower of David's citadel at the Jaffa gate and a corner of the city wall.

a. The rock pinnacle of Golgotha (ringed) now enclosed by the Holy Sepulchre church.

b. The Dome of the Spirits (ringed), formerly the rock in the Holy of Holies of the Temple.

c. The Golden Gate. To the east of it (shaded) is the line of the former causeway over the Kidron valley to the Mount of Olives.

d. Corner of the tower of David's citadel at the Jaffa Gate.

e. Absalom's Tomb.

f. Corner of city wall.

g. Site of Hadrian's column. Roman streets meeting there at angles of 36 degrees give a clue to the pentagonal pattern over the Old City.

g-h. Cardo maximus.

H. Junction of Cardo and Decumanus (east-west).

i-j. Christian Quarter Street.

Details of Jerusalem's topography in Roman and early Christian times were recorded in a sixth-century mosaic discovered in a church at Madaba in Jordan. Most clearly shown is the Cardo, lined with columns and running north (left) to

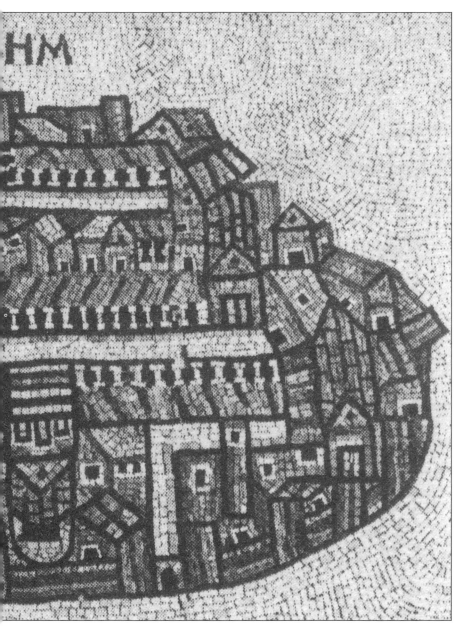

Hadrian's pillar just inside the Damascus gate. Half way down this street is Constantine's church of the Holy Sepulchre which had its façade and main entrance on the Cardo. Behind it in the far, eastern wall is the Golden gate.

paths or ways of the dead. This line, the messianic axis, is traditionally a pathway for souls on their way to paradise; but it is also a triumphal way by which some power or godlike being will enter Jerusalem in glory. The coming is from the east, by the straight path over the Mount of Olives to the Golden gate. Legends and Biblical allusions to the Gate emphasize the greatness and holiness of the one who shall enter by it, and Psalm 24, 9-10 provides the name. "Lift up your heads, O ye gates; even lift them up, ye everlasting doors; and the King of glory shall come in. Who is this King of glory? The Lord of hosts, he is the King of glory."

Rulers and messiahs may display their powers by passing into Jerusalem through the Golden gate – if ever they can persuade it to open. The prophets of old Israel, however, were not speaking of a mortal power but of a divine Prince or King of Glory as the one who shall enter through the gate and to whom the holy city will once again be consecrated. The form and nature of that event are now unimaginable, but a likely portent is the current revelation of the Temple, and that revelation proceeds directly from the newly-recognized 'messianic axis' through Jerusalem.

The pattern over the city

The Old City of Jerusalem can be seen as one large temple. Religion is its main business. Within its ancient, golden stone walls is a labyrinth of narrow alleys, crowded by day with traders, pilgrims and visitors of all types and nations. Jerusalem is unique among holy cities as a sanctuary of not just one but three world-wide religions, Jewish, Christian and Islamic, which compete among themselves for the same sacred places but in normal times are peacefully coexistent. This, sad to say, is largely because the authorities do not allow violence between them. The city's present administrator is the state of Israel, but whoever governs Jerusalem has the historical responsibility, and privilege, of protecting its shrines and pilgrims – and of keeping the peace between its rival sects and religions.

Since Roman times Jerusalem has been divided into four quarters, now called Christian (north-west), Muslim (north-east), Jewish (south-east) and Armenian (south-west). Their borders are still more or less defined by the two main thoroughfares laid out by architects of the Emperor Hadrian, beginning in 135 AD when the city was largely rebuilt on the rubble of its destruction during the suppression of Bar-Kochba's Jewish revolt against Roman rule. The new city was called Aelia Capitolina. It was designed by Roman augurs who used their mysterious craft (a ritual code of town and country planning supposedly inherited from the Etruscans) to bring order and good fortune to cities and settlements.

Laid out by Roman surveyors as broad thoroughfares, Jerusalem's old streets have dwindled to alleys and tunnels. This section of the Via Dolorosa, from St Stephen's gate to the Holy Sepulchre, is still much the same as in W.H. Bartlett's 19th-century illustration.

First they laid down a north-south axis, which they called the Cardo maximus and regarded as a symbol of the universal pole. Then, at right angles to it, they made a cross-axis known as the Decumanus maximus, and built smaller streets parallel to these. At Jerusalem the Cardo was a broad street running southward from the Damascus gate on the line of the present, much reduced Khan al-Zait street. Crossing it at right angles was the Decumanus, represented today by the approximate alignment of David and Chain streets. The lines of these streets perpetuated earlier features; the Cardo was built on or alongside a section of the city's old Western wall (the so-called Second wall), and the Decumanus ran parallel to the east-west orientation of the First wall.

Together with this street grid there is another, set at an angle of about 5 degrees from the first. Its north-south orientation is parallel to the western wall of the Temple Mount, and its east-west line is parallel to the southern wall. Conforming to it are the streets of the Via Dolorosa, beginning at St Stephen's gate to the east.

Just inside the Damascus gate, at the northern terminus of the Cardo, Hadrian's town-planners erected a tall pillar dedicated to the Emperor. It marked the terminus of the Cardo and two other streets, forming angles of 36 degrees and thus conforming to neither of the two rectilinear grids. These streets play an important part in the remarkable geometric scheme which the Roman augurs laid out over the northern half of Jerusalem.

The pole and axis of the whole design of that pattern is the invisible 'messianic line' through the Golden Gate, the former Temple and Golgotha. Parallel to it, 360 cubits (622.08 feet or 189.61 metres) to the south, is the extended axis line through the temple identified by Tuvia Sagiv. It is also the line of the Roman Decumanus. It runs between the northern edge of Absalom's pillar and the corner of the tower of David's citadel at the Jaffa gate, a distance of 2000 cubits. From the angle at the Jaffa gate a perpendicular line, drawn northwards, ends at an angle of the city wall at a point exactly 360 cubits north of the main axis. From that point a line eastward forms the northern side of a rectangle with the messianic line down its centre. This northern side runs parallel to the north wall of the Temple Mount. The eastern side of the rectangle is marked by the east wall at the Golden gate. The dimensions of the rectangle are 720 by 1728 cubits. Measured by the longer 'cubit and a handsbreadth' of 2.0736 feet, these same dimensions are 600 by 1440.

This rectangle provides the framework for the grid of streets in the north-west quarter of the city, now called the Christian quarter. One of its streets, Christian Quarter Street, conforms to this grid, lying parallel to and exactly half way between the western side of the rectangle and the main north-south Cardo. The messianic line at right angles to that street divides the area of the rectangle west of the Cardo into four smaller rectangles, each of 300 x 360 cubits, and the extension of the line to its terminus near the most western point of the city wall is another 300 cubits.

To the east of the Cardo, in the Muslim quarter, the other street-grid takes over. In contrast to the east-west axis of the first grid, the main orientation of the second is north-south, parallel to the line of the western wall of the Temple Mount. This orientation has its own axis, which is formed by the street line from the north of the Temple Mount, projected southward through the sacred enclosure and passing over the Dome of the Rock, the El Kas fountain and the Aqsa mosque (see plan, page 56).

An example of the symbolism inherent in Jerusalem's street pattern is provided by those prominent streets that do not conform to either of the two grids. These are the streets that radiate from the site of Hadrian's column inside the Damascus Gate, forming angles of 36 degrees. This is an angle of the pentagon and five-pointed star. When the pentagon is duly completed, with the five-pointed star inside it, it is found to be centred upon the messianic line, which forms its axis, and each of its sides measures 720 cubits, the same length as the shorter sides of the framework rectangle.

The north-south diagonal of the pentagon falls upon the line of the main street in the Old City, the Cardo. The symmetry of the scheme suggests another, reciprocal pentagon, 'married' to the first and sharing its north-south diagonal. Resulting from their union is a figure with six equal sides of 720 cubits. In Pythagorean number symbolism six is known as the marriage number, and the symbolism of this particular figure, the marriage of equal pentagons, is natural and obvious. It demonstrates reconciliation, and since the pentagon is

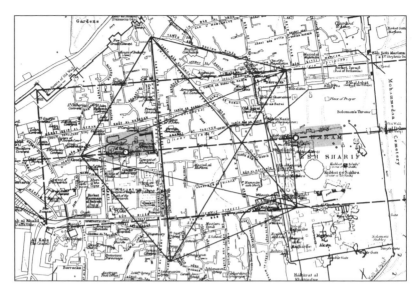

The pentagon pattern developed from the lines of streets meeting inside the Damascus gate at angles of 36 degrees.

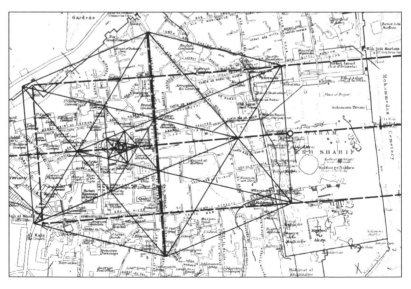

The reciprocal pentagon, conjoined with the first with their common axis on the line of the Cardo. A series of reducing pentagrams at the centre of the western pentagon pinpoints the location of Golgotha.

the equally natural symbol of humanity, the reconciliation here is between two nations or peoples. Whoever designed this pattern put into it every possible indication of their purpose, to represent, and thus magically procure, harmony between two different peoples living and worshipping in the same city.

The subtle beauty of the designers' geomantic art is illustrated in a detail of the second, western pentagon. Its diagonals create a smaller pentagon at its centre; within that can be drawn a lesser pentagon, and so on, down to the central dot. In this case, the dot at the centre of the reducing pentagons is the rock of Golgotha.

A five-pointed star with a dot (Golgotha?) at its centre and with the Hebrew letters, J, R, S, L, M, placed around it is an ancient emblem of the spiritual Jerusalem. This example from a vessel of the second or third century is illustrated in Tuvia Sagiv's book, Penetrating Insights into the Temple Mount.

The Temple revealed

Readers who have come so far may already have anticipated this revelation. All the clues are there, and once they are put together the truth becomes obvious. It is that the rectangle, stretching across the newer, northern part of the Old City, forms the outline of a large-scale temple. It is a recognizable temple, a magnification of that temple which Kaufman found and measured on the Temple Mount. The dimensions he published (63.4 x 151.6 metres) show that its overall measures were, width 120 cubits, length 288 cubits, a ratio of 5 to 12. When these dimensions are multiplied by six, making them 720 by 1728 cubits, the enlarged plan fits perfectly into the plan of the city and its 720-by-1728-cubit rectangle.

The whole greater temple is based upon two rocks, Golgotha, the most sacred rock of Christianity, and the Rock of Foundation on which the Ark rested in the Holy of Holies of the Temple. These two rocks are symmetrically placed within the temple rectangle, the same distance from each end, and they divide its axis into four equal parts, each of 432 cubits. They have determined the entire shape and plan of the northern quarters of the Old City. They are indeed the twin pillars and foundation stones of Jerusalem's greater temple.

In the greater temple the Golden gate forms the eastern entrance, leading into the outer court. The magnified version of the Hekhal stands with its front upon the Cardomaximus, on the site of Constantine's

Holy Sepulchre church. Golgotha appears as an altar within the Holy Place, and the Holy of Holies falls to the west of the church. The entire city with its shrines, mosques, synagogues and churches is revealed as one temple, which is how it actually is.

This greater temple of Jerusalem is alluded to by Old Testament and Christian prophets, and they are united in seeing it as for 'all nations'. It is that predetermined temple, always located in the future, which is not just for one people, one religion and one set of rituals, but accommodates them all, just as they are. It is a temple of the spirit, seen by the spiritual eye, invisible to the grosser faculties. It has no cult or priesthood of its own, no property or possessions, nor does it demand tribute from the separate religions in Jerusalem, to all of whom it gives protection. The protection it gives is not material but something firmer and more needed. In the Holy City today, and the land around it, peace is maintained by force of arms in an atmosphere of fear and hatred. It would take a miracle to change that. But revelations are miracles, and the revelation of Jerusalem as the promised temple for all people can so utterly change hearts and minds that the miracle may happen, delivering the Land of Israel from the rule of fear and bringing to mind its true nature as the Holy Land.

This is the temple of prophecy, as foreseen by the Biblical sages. Ezekiel in his detailed description of the Temple's dimensions uses two different scales of measure, the Hebrew cubit and the rod of six cubits,

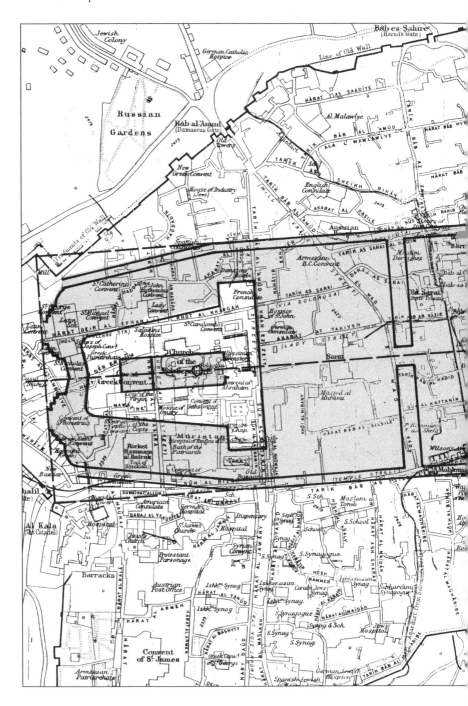

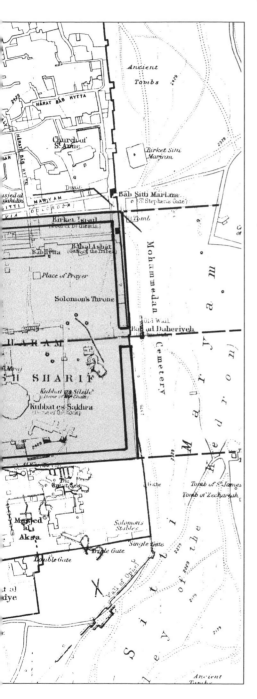

*Kaufman's temple plan, with its
dimensions multiplied by six, fits the
outline of the greater temple rectangle,
and correlates with the hidden geometry
in the Old City plan. In this magnified
temple the east-facing front of the main
sanctuary, the Hekhal, stands upon the
Cardo, and the entrance to the outer,
eastern court of the greater temple is
represented by the Golden Gate. The
dimensions of this greater temple are
720 x 1728 cubits, which is six times
larger that the 120 x 288 cubits of the
former Temple. The value of the cubit is
1.728 feet.*

implying the 1 to 6 ratio between the actual building and the greater temple over the city. Isaiah makes it plain that the future Temple will not belong only to one people but will admit the "sons of the stranger", and he writes (56, 7) "For my house shall be an house of prayer for all people". The prophet Haggai saw further than the Second Temple when he proclaimed that "the glory of this latter House shall be greater than of the former". He too envisaged the future temple as a universal sanctuary:

"And I will shake all nations, and the desire of all nations shall come: and I will fill this House with glory, says the Lord of Hosts." - Haggai, 2, 7.

This is repeated by other prophets.

"The mountain of the Lord's house shall be established in the top of the mountains... and all nations shall flow unto it." - Isaiah, 2, 2.

"They shall call Jerusalem the throne of the Lord; and all nations shall be gathered unto it." - Jeremiah, 3, 17.

This same theme is continued in the New Testament. St John in his vision of the heavenly city sees that the New Jerusalem is not focused upon any particular building. Inhabited by the Holy Spirit, the city itself will be the temple. In Revelation, 21, he says:

"And I saw no temple therein: for the Lord God Almighty and the Lamb are the temple of it. And the nations of them which are saved shall walk in the light of it: and the kings of the earth do bring their glory and honour into it. And the gates of it shall not be shut at all by day: for there shall be no night there. And they shall bring the glory and honour of the nations into it."

At the centre of the new, revealed Jerusalem, John sees no temple but the Tree of Life, bearing twelve different kinds of fruit (an image from Ezekiel, 47, 12).

"And he showed me a pure river of water of life, clear as crystal, proceeding out of the throne of God and of the Lamb. In the midst of the street of it, and on either side of the river, was there the tree of life, which bare twelve manner of fruits, and yielded her fruit every month: and the leaves of the tree were for the healing of the nations." Revelation, 22, 1-2.

In the last words of his final chapter Ezekiel gives a name to the twelve-gated holy city. It is called, he says, 'The Lord is there'.

The clear message of prophecy is that the holy city of Jerusalem will become the new Temple and that the twelve tribes of Israel will gather there, preparing the way for the Millennium and God's rule upon earth. An outcome of that process is the 'healing of the nations'. Above its literal meaning, Israel is a symbol of sanctified humanity, and its twelve tribes represent the twelve different nations or types of personality into which humanity is traditionally divided.

The measures and numbers of the Temple

The plan of the Temple as revealed to King David was, like the plan of the Tabernacle that preceded it, a composition of proportions and harmonies that represented the structure of the universe. It was measured by certain 'sacred' units, all related to the foot as used today, and also related to the dimensions of the earth. Describing his vision of the Temple, the prophet Ezekiel mentioned three units in its dimensions: the cubit, the cubit-and-a-handsbreadth or greater cubit and the reed of six greater cubits. These are:

i. the cubit of 1.728 ft. The duodecimal aspect of this unit (1728 = 12 x 12 x 12) is, of course, only apparent when its length is expressed in feet. This is the canonical Egyptian cubit of which there are 1750 around the base of the Great Pyramid and 12,096,000 in the earth's mean radius. It is made up of 5 handsbreadths or hands. The hand of 0.3456 ft, a version of which is still used for the measurement of horses, corresponds to the measure across the knuckles on the back of the hand from the joint of the thumb to the base of the little finger. The hand contains 5 digits or finger-widths.

A cubit is one and a half feet, so the foot belonging to this cubit is the canonical Egyptian of 1.152 ft. This is the unit by which the Temple Mount was planned (see page 68).

ii. the cubit and a handsbreadth or Hebrew cubit of 2.0736 ft = 12 x 12 x 12 x 12/10000 feet. It is made up of 6 hands and therefore relates to the canonical cubit as 6 to 5. This cubit of 6 hands is the 'medium' cubit that Kaufman identifies from the Mishnah Kélim 17, 9, as the principal unit in the Temple plan. In Ezekiel 41, 8, it is called the great cubit.

Another small unit, the palm, contains 4 digits and therefore relates to the hand as 4 to 5. The 6-palm cubit of 1.65888 ft that derives from it is called Sumerian and can also be found in the Temple dimensions.

iii. the reed of 6 great cubits or 12.4416 ft. In Ezekiel 40, the prophet encounters a mystical surveyor bearing a rod of this length for measuring the Temple and its precincts. It is called "a full reed of six great cubits". The great cubit measures the Temple itself, while the reed measures the greater temple across Jerusalem whose dimensions are six times greater than those of the actual building. Thus the width of the former Temple, as given by Ezekiel, is 100 great cubits and its length is 240 great cubits, whereas the dimensions of the greater temple are 100 by 240 reeds.

In summary,

Egyptian canonical cubit = 5 hands = 1.728 ft = 0.526694 metres.

Hebrew great cubit = 6 hands = 2.0736 ft = 0.6320328 metres.

reed = 36 hands = 12.4416 ft = 3.7921968 metres.

These units are plainly indicated in the greater temple over Jerusalem by the distance between its two pillars, the Rock of Foundation in the old Temple and the rock of Golgotha. They stand on the main axis 455.064 metres apart, meaning that the distance between them is

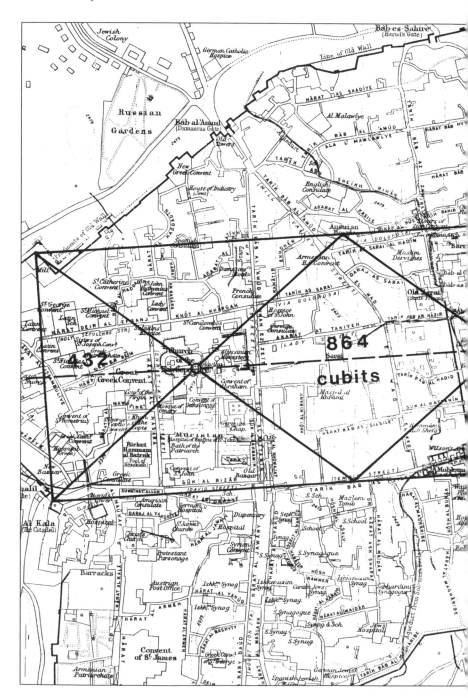

Within the greater temple rectangle the two sacred rocks, Golgotha and the Rock of Foundation, are symmetrically placed and divide the axis into four equal sections of 432 cubits. The distance between the two rocks is 864 cubits, a 14,000th part of the earth's mean radius.

864 Egyptian or 720 Hebrew cubits or 120 full reeds. Since both these rocks are natural outcrops, it can be said that nature herself provides the yardstick for measuring the temple.

It is also the yardstick for measuring the Earth. The distance between the two rocks is precisely one fourteen thousandth part of the Earth's mean radius, the distance from its centre to the surface. These are the figures:

864 cubits of 1.728 feet, multiplied by 14000, are equal to 12096000 cubits or:

20901888 feet;

6370890 metres;

Earth's mean radius.

The various and numerous units of ancient metrology are called for convenience Roman, Greek, Egyptian, Hebrew and so on, but such names are arbitrary because all these units are part of one system and relate to each other by simple ratios. Their world-wide unity indicates that they are older than any civilization known to history. The 'stranger' among units of length today is the metre. It was defined by French scientists at the end of the 18th century to represent a forty-millionth part of the earth's mean circumference, the ancient and true reckoning of which is 24883.2 or a tenth part of 12 x 12 x 12 x 12 x 12 miles. This is equivalent to 40,045,590 metres. If only the scientists had studied ancient metrology, they would have framed their new unit in conformity with ancient standards and thus made it geodetically accurate.

The dimensions of the former Temple are:

1440 by 600 handsbreadths of 0.3456 ft.

288 by 120 Egyptian canonical cubits of 1.728 ft.

240 by 100 Hebrew great cubits of 2.0736 ft.

These, multiplied by 6, give the dimensions of the greater temple:

8640 by 3600 handsbreadths;

1728 by 720 Egyptian canonical cubits;

1440 by 600 Hebrew greater cubits;

240 by 100 reeds.

The number of feet in the length of the greater temple is 2985.984 or a thousandth part of 12 x 12 x 12 x 12 x 12 x 12 feet.

The use of two different cubits (1.728 and 2.0736 feet) continues the theme of reconciliation that characterizes the Jerusalem scheme. The ratio of 10:12 is emphasized throughout. It determines the proportions of the greater temple rectangle whose sides are 720 by 1728 cubits, a ratio of 10:24, and it occurs in the block of four rectangles, formed by the parallel streets and the main axis in the area west of the Cardo. This can be seen on the map. page 28. The sides of these rectangles are as 10 to 12, measuring 300 by 360 lesser cubits or 250 by 300 in the greater units. The interplay here is between the numbers 10 and 12. There is a natural tension between these numbers and between the decimal and duodecimal systems of counting and measuring. Both have their own advantages, but whereas ten is the most apparently convenient base, number itself is essentially duodecimal. That is why the circle is divided into 360 degrees – a convention of unknown origin and very great antiquity. In Plato's allegory of Atlantis, one reason for its fall was that it was founded on decimal number, in contrast to his

The pool of Bethesda (Birkat Israel) was made as part of Herod's temple works to supply water to the sanctuary. It has now been filled in. Its southern wall, shown here in W.H Bartlett's woodcut of 1867, formed part of the north wall of the Temple Mount.

ideal city whose plan and constitution were in units of twelve. In the Jerusalem scheme, decimal and duodecimal numbers are woven together, as if to symbolize harmony between those who count and measure in tens and the less obvious but more arithmetically natural base of twelve.

The number 864 is prominent in the temple measures, in the 864-cubit distance between the two sacred rocks and in the 8640 hands (equal to 1728 Egyptian or 1440 Hebrew cubits) in the length of the greater temple. In a previous work (John Michell, *The Dimensions of Paradise*, 1988) a short essay on this number identifies its symbolism.

"In the language of symbolic number, 864 pertains to a centre of radiant energy, the sun in the solar system, Jerusalem on earth, the inner sanctuary of the temple, the altar... and the corner stone on which the whole sacred edifice is founded."

The diameter of the sun is 864 thousand miles, four hundred times greater than the canonical 2160 miles in the moon's diameter. 864 is called the 'foundation number'; in the gematria of New Testament Greek, 864 corresponds to words or phrases such as 'altar', 'corner stone', 'sanctuary of the gods', 'holy of holies' and, most strikingly in this context, 'Jerusalem'. The sum of the numerical values of the ten Greek letters in 'Jerusalem' is:

Iota 10 + epsilon 5 + rho 100 + omicron 70 + upsilon 400+ sigma 200 + alpha 1 + lamda 30 + eta 8 + mu 40 = 864.

In Ezekiel's temple the altar is described as a square of 12 x 12 cubits. Its height is not given, but since the traditional altar was conceived of as a cube, half of it above ground and half below, it was presumably 6 cubits, so the measure of the altar in cubic cubits was 864. The surface area of the six sides of a cube of 12 is also 864.

There is much more to be discovered on the numbers, measures and geometric symbolism in the Jerusalem temple plan. This revelation inevitably draws attention to that ancient code of sacred science which was suppressed by the three monotheistic religions. The greater temple of Jerusalem could provide the focus for its revival.

The temple of the four directions

When the dimensions of Kaufman's Temple are
multiplied by six, and his diagram is placed with the
same orientation within the Jerusalem rectangle, the
principal holy places in this greater Temple fall upon the
Holy Sepulchre, the most holy church in Christendom,
on the traditional site where Jesus was executed and
entombed. Religious Jews may find this inappropriate
and even impious, but Christian occupation of these sites
is a quite recent episode in Jerusalem's long history. Up
to 334 a Roman temple to Venus occupied the site of the
Holy Sepulchre, and a statue of the goddess stood on top
of Golgotha. Judaism is older than Christianity,
Jerusalem as a settlement is even older and the rock of
Golgotha is older still. Archaeologists have evidence that
Golgotha was a prehistoric altar or focus of ritual. One of
its impressive legends is that Adam's skull, taken by Noah
into the Ark, was finally buried beneath it by his son,
Shem. That is why it is called Golgotha (latinized as
Calvary) meaning 'place of the skull'. To followers of the
Bible this makes it a natural world-centre. Golgotha is
likely to have been the ritual centre for the Jews before
Solomon built the Temple and relocated the centre in its
sanctum. It must be older than the rediscovered site of
the Rock of Foundation, because it is a natural rock
pillar, while the other is a featureless patch of bedrock at
a spot which happened to be on the right axis and 864
cubits distant from Golgotha. From the pivot of Golgotha
the ancient surveyors measured the city, adding another

pivot, the rock in Solomon's Temple. This second pivot became the Israelites' sacred centre rather than the first, but whoever laid out the symmetrical pattern, now recognized as the greater plan of the Temple, restored the balance by giving the two rocks equal importance in the scheme. The bifocal design was clearly intended to represent harmony between two different religions.

Nor is that the end of the matter. The Jerusalem street pattern has two main axis lines. One is the east-west line of the 'messianic axis', orientated about 5 degrees north of east, and the other is angled 10 degrees west of north. This north-south axis runs parallel to the western wall of the Temple Mount and through its principal Muslim shrines, continuing south through the Double gate which gave access to the Temple area in Biblical times. It was probably the cross-axis of Solomon's Temple. That is the conclusion of Temple researcher David Jacobson, who locates Solomon's Holy Place on the site of the Dome of the Rock.

Tuvia Sagiv believes that this north-south axis was also that of the former Roman temple dedicated to Jupiter, Juno and Minerva. After the destruction of Herod's temple in the year 70, the Romans built a large pagan temple across its site. Temples in the ancient world were normally orientated more or less to the east, towards the point of sunrise on a particular day. An example is the Jupiter temple at Baalbek, which was erected by the same architect and at much the same time as the Jerusalem building. There were, however, certain exceptions to this rule. Temples which, for reasons

The north-south axis through the Muslim shrines, on which the temple of Jupiter was probably located, runs parallel to the western wall of the Haram al-Sharif, at right angles to its southern side and at the same angle as the grid of streets to the north and west. The line continues through the ancient Double gate (closed for about a thousand years) to one of Jerusalem's oldest sites, near the Gihon spring where Solomon was annointed king. On this line, inscribed above the Double gate, is a Roman dedication to the Emperor Hadrian, addressed as "the Prophet-Priest". This inscription is believed to be a relic of the temple of Jupiter, marking its axis.

evidently connected with astronomy and geomancy, were orientated in other directions, including to the north, are discussed by Jean Richer in *Sacred Geography of the Ancient Greeks*. Sagiv believes that the Jupiter temple on the Temple platform was aligned north-south. When he laid the scaled plan of the Baalbek temple over the Temple Mount, he found that its main features coincided with the present pattern of Muslim sites. The basilica would have been on the site of the Aqsa mosque, with a polygonal structure on the place now occupied by the octagonal Dome of the Rock. Sagiv's view is that the temple of Jupiter was converted to Christian use in the fourth century, and when Islam arose in the seventh century, it became the foundation for their sacred buildings. The same axis was retained because the same pagan line to the north also ran south towards Mecca.

There are not just three but four religions with historical rights and claims on Jerusalem, but three of them are united in despising and excluding the fourth, that religion of philosophers that maintained classical civilization under the twelve gods. Jews and Christians claim many martyrs from persecutions by the classical religion, but when their turn came they and the Muslims persecuted it to extinction and have reviled the name of paganism ever since. That of course was not the situation when the unknown planners of Jerusalem's street pattern executed their work. The reconciliation that idealists of that time would have had in mind was between Jews and classicists. Christians and Muslims came later, but when they came they found the two

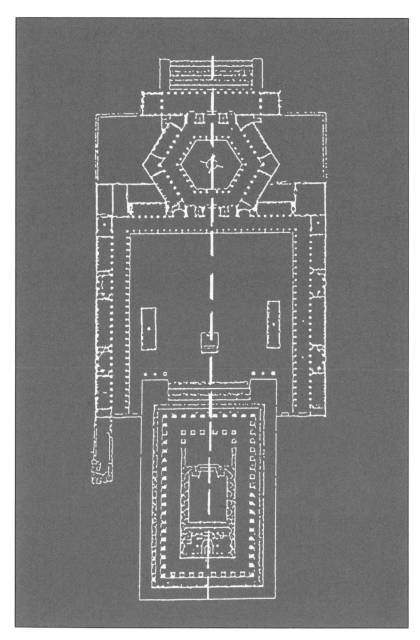

The plan of the Roman temple of Jupiter at Baalbek (above) is similar to the pattern of Muslim shrines on the Temple Mount. This indicates that the Muslim architects in the seventh century followed the orientation of the temple to Jupiter which the

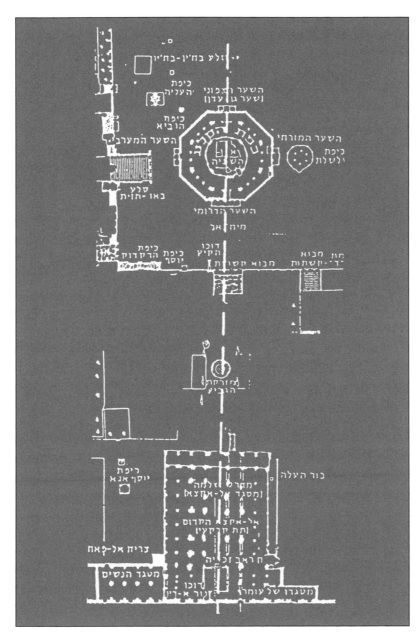

Romans built across the site of the Jews' Temple. Tuvia Sagiv, from whose book these diagrams are reproduced, believes that the First and Second Temples were located on an east-west axis between the Dome of the Rock and the Asqa mosque.

existing axis lines, suitable for their respective purposes, one pointing west towards Rome and the other south towards Mecca. The Holy Sepulchre is rare among Christian churches in having its orientation to the west, towards the tomb of Jesus at its west end. This leaves the city's eastern orientation to the Jews.

Whether by chance or divine intent, Jerusalem has become the temple of four types of religion, issuing like the four rivers of paradise that rose from beneath the Temple towards the four directions, Jews to the east, Muslims to the south, Christians to the west and, in the direction of the north pole, followers of that ancient religious system that preceded the others.

The twelve tribes and the Temple

The revelation of the Temple and the gathering there of the Twelve Tribes of Israel are events which go together. So it is emphasized by the prophets. Yet here arises an immediate difficulty, because the identity of these tribes is now unknown. The Jews claim to represent only two and a part of them – Judah, Benjamin and an 'admixture of Levites'. The others, who never returned from captivity in Assyria in the eighth century BC, are lost among the 'nations of the world'. Sects and nations in all continents have declared themselves or been declared by others as one or more of the lost tribes, and the whole subject has been swamped by antiquarian fantasy.

Once Jerusalem as a whole is understood to be the prophesied Temple, the question can be seen in a new light. This greater temple is not a building exclusive to one expression of religion, but, dedicated to the Almighty, it is the spiritual centre of all who feel drawn to it. And since Jerusalem is Zion, a proper name for spiritual attraction towards Jerusalem is Zionism. This, of course, requires the redefinition of the meaning of Zionism. At present it is conventionally applied to the movement for resettling the Jews in the Holy Land, but it need not be so limited. All who aspire to Zion are by definition Zionists. Those of whatever race or religion, who think of Zion as their spiritual home, have their rightful place in the greater temple of Jerusalem, and by their yearning for Zion they identify themselves as among the lost tribes of Israel.

These present times are times of revelation, so it is not surprising that this perception is already alive in Jerusalem. Its philosopher and promoter is Isaac Hayutman, founder of the Academy of Jerusalem, an institution for studying and teaching current revelations of ancient and forgotten knowledge. With the appearance of the prophesied temple, his insight takes on new significance.

As the temple has revealed itself, so will the twelve tribes. And as the process develops, something else is revealed. The number twelve is a symbol of natural order. Number itself is basically duodecimal. That is why past civilizations have adopted the number twelve as the basis for ordering time, both greater and lesser cycles, for theology, psychology and political constitutions. The dodecahedron with its twelve pentagonal faces was Plato's symbol for the ideal earth, and it is a model for the tradition of twelve races or psychological types of humanity forming a perfect union. In classical Greece each nation with its own cult and sanctuary was divided into twelve tribes, three to each of the four quarters, in imitation of the zodiac. This same cosmological pattern has been known at different times throughout the world. Associated with this pattern is the form of religion which recognizes a council of twelve gods, the Olympians, and draws its teachings from science and philosophy rather than beliefs and dogma. Its worthy followers are initiated in the Mysteries and led towards justice and understanding. They inherit a tradition that goes back to the earliest times and recurs at different periods to provide true standards for human living and to refresh human spirits and culture.

There is a fourth religion that partakes in Jerusalem's revealed temple, and it is the oldest and deepest. It is called pagan, but that is a derogatory name, implying ignorance and superstition, which was given to it by its enemies. Properly styled, it is the classical or philosopher's religion. Truth, wisdom and knowledge (in descending order) are its ideals; it demands no artificial beliefs. And it is unique among religions in being called perenniel - rooted in nature and human nature and so ever recurrent. Like the temple and the regathering of the tribes, the reappearance of this perennial tradition, and the sacred science that comes with it, is a necessary part of the Millennial process.

Zechariah's prophecy of the Messiah (9, 9) is, "Shout, O daughter of Jerusalem: behold, thy King cometh unto thee: he is just, and having salvation; lowly, and riding upon an ass..." Before him will walk the prophet Elijah blowing a shofar. In this picture from an old Hebrew manuscript, the Prophet and the Messiah are approaching the Golden gate along the messianic path from the Mount of Olives. In front of the Gate is a Muslim cemetery, said to be a barrier against Elijah. The Prophet is a Cohen of priestly family, and would therefore be defiled by walking over a grave.

The origin of the Temple pattern

The plan of the Temple, it is said, was divinely revealed to Moses and again to King David, and the more one studies that beautiful scheme the more one is persuaded that the traditional account is the most likely. It explains why the Temple has such enduring power as an image and why it recurs from time to time, in response to need or invocation. The present revelation is not just of the Temple's former site but of its pattern in outline, spread across the old city of Jerusalem and marking it out as a sanctuary which, as the prophets emphasized, is for all nations. It is an awesome disclosure, and it naturally provokes curiosity. How is it that the city has grown over the ages to bear the imprint of a great temple? Who, if anyone, was responsible for it?

Some features of the pattern are old, from the time of the First Temple, but the lay-out of streets and shrines that make it recognizable today is no earlier than the reign of Herod the Great (37- 4 BC); and its most obvious features are the thoroughfares created by the Romans in the second century. Throughout that period, during which Herod's temple was built and destroyed, together with almost the entire city, the development of Jerusalem was evidently guided by a single plan, secretly maintained by generations of architects, masons and augurs. One sign of that is the 'messianic axis'. Its line, about 5 degrees north of east, is parallel to the northern wall of the Temple Mount and was followed by the Roman road-builders. It also defined the orientation of

Herod's temple. Kaufman reckons that Herod's works were aligned due east-west, but this is disputed by other specialists, and the evidence here shows that the line between Golgotha and the Dome of the Spirits was the main axis on which Jerusalem was planned over a period which coincided with the birth and rise of Christianity.

The key to Jerusalem's street pattern with its two different orientations is in the Temple Mount (see Addendum). Its vast raised platform, concealing many subterranean mysteries, was the preliminary work for Herod's temple, from about 22 BC. None of its four walls are parallel, but at two corners, north-east and south-west, they form right angles. The north wall, and the northern section of the east wall, are aligned with the messianic axis and the Roman street works; the walls on the west and south sides conform to the other orientation of streets, 10 degrees east of north. This second orientation has been identified as that of Solomon's temple, preserved by Herod's architects in their rebuilding of the Temple Mount. Its north-south line survives today as the axis of the Muslim sacred places.

The following conclusion is offered lightly, because it is really no more than an impression. It is that the pattern over Jerusalem that is now emerging - the pattern of a greater temple that accommodates all twelve tribes - was revealed and given shape at around the beginning of the Christian era. It was worked upon by a succession of mystical idealists, Jews, Romans and others, motivated by the millennial spirit of that time, the spirit that gave birth to Christianity.

The history of early Christianity has been so thoroughly and purposefully mythologized that there is no true record of how it arose and how it affected the people of Jerusalem at the time. Jesus as a person has been idealized beyond recognition; even his name was adapted to produce (by the sum of the numerical correspondents of the Greek letters comprising it) the number 888. That is affirmed by gnostic writers and by Irenaeus among the early Christian fathers. Only in St John's Revelation is there a hint of the millennial fervour that settled upon Jerusalem at the time of Jesus and was later called the spirit of Christianity. Herod was then King of the Jews, but he was subject to the Romans, and everything he did, including his temple building, was by Roman consent. A picture that comes into view is of a priestly guild or freemasonry of architects, influenced by the millennial outburst that became identified with Christianity, designing a temple and a pattern of streets as clues to the Secret of Jerusalem. That secret is nothing less than the temple that Solomon spread out over Jerusalem, his universal temple, his sanctuary of the Twelve Tribes or of all those who accept Jerusalem as their spiritual centre.

This is a deep and mystical subject. There is no doubt, according to the Bible, that Solomon's overall temple plan was not only for the Jews but for all the nations from which his wives and concubines were drawn - meaning for all nations. That plan, the pattern of the greater temple over Jerusalem, was referred to by

Ezekiel and other ancient prophets. St John also knew the secret, for at the beginning of Revelation 21 he identifies the visionary city of Jerusalem with the temple and proclaims that it is already here.

"Behold, the tabernacle of God is with men, and he will dwell with them, and they shall be his people."

So here is mystery. The lack of any good, rational alternative leaves room for the miraculous: that the wonderful pattern over the Holy City was a product of divine providence, working through each generation of various different peoples to create an active symbol of the Holy Spirit that is ever the same for everyone, everywhere. The revelation of that pattern was to come about when it was needed, in response to a generation's desire for the 'healing of nations', and in God's good time. It seems likely that the time has come.

Addendum

Writing about something is like an invocation; the subject floods in on you. Since this work was started, certain facts have emerged on the geometry, measures and cosmological symbolism of the Temple Mount, opening new lines of research into the mysteries of Jerusalem. For the interest of those involved in this subject, here are some of the main points.

From published measures of the four walls of the Temple Mount it is apparent that the principal unit of measure in their planning was not the familiar cubit of 1.728 ft, but the foot belonging to that cubit. A cubit is one and a half feet, so the foot in this case is the Egyptian unit of 1.152 ft. In terms of this unit the lengths of the walls are: N. 880; E. 1320; S. 800; W. 1400. The total length of the perimeter is therefore 4400 Egyptian feet. This is equal to 1545 metres which compares well over this distance with the published figure of 1546.15 metres.

The north wall measures a fifth part of the perimeter and the other walls are in proportion to it, most notably the west wall whose 1400 Egyptian feet, multiplied by 22/7, gives the perimeter of 4400. The perimeter is therefore equal in length to the circumference of a circle whose diameter is the length of the west wall. This is the same style of geometry as in the Great Pyramid, whose height is equal to the radius of a circle with its circumference equal to the measure round the four base sides. It fulfills the requirement of every sacred foundation - ancient Rome for example - that its basic pattern should be of an equal square and circle, symbolizing the union of spirit and matter.

The geodetic significance of the 1400 Egyptian feet (1612.8 English feet) in the west wall is that, when multiplied by 12960 (a hundredth part of the number of seconds in a circle), the result is 20901888 ft, the canonical figure for the earth's mean radius. Similarly, the distance round the four walls multiplied by 12960 produces the meridian, the surface distance between the earth's two poles.

The internal arrangement of the Temple Mount is rich in symbolic proportions. David Jacobson opened the subject with his observation that a perpendicular from the mid-point of the west wall, extended eastwards, runs through the centre of the Dome of the Rock and the Dome of the Chain beyond it. A point within this smaller dome marks the centrepoint of the whole scheme; a circle drawn from it touches the four corners of the Temple enclosure.

Developing here is a vast new area of research, promising not just archaeological discoveries but those greater rewards which tradition associates with the revelation of Solomon's Temple.

Acknowledgements

To Christine Rhone, co-author with John Michell of *Twelve-Tribe Nations* in which an earlier version of this essay formed a chapter. She has drawn the plans and diagrams in this book - which is a guarantee of their meticulous accuracy.

To Isaac Hayutman, founder of the Academy of Jerusalem, whose hospitality in the Old City made this book possible, whose inspiration was contagious and whose expert guidance kept us on the straight path.

To Asher Kaufman for permitting reproduction of his two Temple groundplans; to him and Tuvia Sagiv for generously sharing knowledge and insights and for encouraging this work.

To Gordon Strachan, Christopher Gibbs, Susan Rose, friends and helpers in the Holy Land.

Maps

The Israel Survey Department supplied an up-to-date 1: 2500 map of Jerusalem's Old City, from which measurements and other data in this book were obtained. This and all later surveys were derived from that of Captain (later Sir Charles) Wilson, published in 1865. The engraved version, used here, is from G.A. Smith's *Atlas of the Historical Geography of the Holy Land*, 1915.

Literary sources

This work is not based on extensive reading, so this is not a representative bibliography of the subject but a list of books and articles that have been found useful or are mentioned in the text.

Bahat, Dan. *Carta's Historical Atlas of Jerusalem*. Jerusalem, 1998.

Bartlett, W.H. *Jerusalem Revisited*. London, 1867.

Cohn, Erich W. *New Ideas about Jerusalem's Topography*. Jerusalem, 1987.

Freeman-Grenville, G.S.P. *The Beauty of Jerusalem*. London, 1983.

— 'The Basilica of the Holy Sepulchre'. *Journal of the Royal Asiatic Society*. London, 1987.

Har-el, Menashe. *This is Jerusalem*. Jerusalem, 1977.

Hayutman, Isaac. Academy of Jerusalem publications, PO Box 8115, Jerusalem 91080.

Jacobson, David. 'Sacred Geometry - Unlocking the Secrets of the Temple Mount'. *Biblical Archaeology Review*. Washington, DC, July/August and September/October 1999.

Kaufman, Asher S. *The Temple of Jerusalem, Part 1: Tractate Middot* (in Hebrew with English summary and captions to diagrams). Jerusalem, 1991.

— 'New Light upon Zion: the plan and precise location of the Second Temple'. *Ariel*, no. 43. Jerusalem, 1977.

'Where the Ancient Temple of Jerusalem stood.' *Biblical Archaeology Review*. Washington, DC, March/April 1983.

— 'New Light on the Ancient Temple of Jerusalem'. *Christian News in Israel*, XXVI. Jerusalem, 1978.

— 'The Temple and Subterranean Structures in the Temple Area'. *BDD, Journal of Torah and Scholarship*. Israel, Summer 1998.

— and Leen Ritmeyer. 'Where Was the Temple?' *Biblical Archaeology Review*. Washington, DC, March/April 2000.

Klein, Herbert A. *Temple Beyond Time*. Malibu, CA, 1986.

Lev, Martin. *The Traveler's Key to Jerusalem*. New York, 1989.

Michell, John. *Ancient Metrology*. Bristol, 1981.

— *The Dimentions of Paradise*. London, 1988.

— and Christine Rhone. *Twelve-Tribe Nations*. London, 1991.

Patai, Raphael. *Man and Temple in Ancient Jewish Myth and Ritual*. London, 1947.

Prag, Kay. *Blue Guide to Jerusalem*. London & New York, 1989.

Richer, Jean. *Sacred Geography of the Ancient Greeks* (tr. Christine Rhone). Albany, NY, 1994.

Ritmeyer, Leen and Kathleen. *Secrets of Jerusalem's Temple Mount*. Washington, DC, 1998.

Sagiv Shekerka, Tuvia. *Temples on Mount Moriah*. Tel Aviv, 1998.

Vilnay, Zev. *Legends of Jerusalem*. Philadelphia, 1973.

Index